# Handy Connecticut Genealogy Handbook

I0450159

## Gary L. Morris

©2015 Gary L. Morris

ISBN-13: 978-1507746226

ISBN-10: 1507746229

Table of Contents

# Notes

**Genealogical Research in Connecticut**

Connecticut has a long and colourful history, making it especially interesting to conduct research in the state. While researching Connecticut genealogy records presents a unique set of challenges; it also has its own unique rewards. There are many historical and genealogical records available for the state, and we know just where to find them. To get you started in tracing your ancestry, we'll introduce you to those records, and help you to understand:

       1.     What they are
       2.     Where to find them
       3.     How to use them

These records can be found both online and off, so we'll introduce you to online websites, indexes and databases, as well as brick-and-mortar repositories and other institutions that will help with your research in Connecticut. So that you will have a more comprehensive understanding of these records, we have provided a brief history of the "Constitution State" to illustrate what type of records may have been generated during specific time periods. That information will assist you in pinpointing times and locations on which to focus the search for your Connecticut ancestors and their records.

## A Brief History of Connecticut

Connecticut as we know it today was first settled by Europeans when the Dutch built a small fort on the site of modern day Hartford. As English settler began to move into the area the Dutch abandoned their post and members of the Plymouth colony established a settlement on the site of Windsor in 1633.

European settlement was resisted by the Native Pequot tribe which led to their defeat by the English in the Pequot War of 1637. In 1643 the New England Confederation, an informal union for mutual defences was formed when New Haven and Connecticut colonies united with the Massachusetts Bay colony. Connecticut won its legal right to exist as a corporate colony when Governor John Winthrop secured a royal charter in 1662.

Connecticut continued to grow through the seventeenth century, yet by the mid 18th century a bitter feud had developed between conservatives and radicals in the colony. During the Revolutionary War Connecticut served as the chief supply area for the continental Army, and several towns such as Danbury, New Haven, New London, and Fairfield were attacked by the British.

After the Revolutionary War Connecticut prospered, its ports bustling with business and textile mills thriving. In 1788 Connecticut became the 5th US State, even though opposing the foreign policy of presidents Thomas Jefferson and James Madison. Connecticut opposed the War of 1812, going as far as refusing to allow its militia to leave the state. The War 12 severely hurt exports, though the end result promoted rapid growth of industry.

Connecticut had very strong anti-slavery sentiments, enacting legislation that any slave that every black born after 1 March 1784 would be free at age 25. The state finally abolished slavery in 1848. There was no question about supporting the union cause during the Civil War, and Connecticut sent almost 60,000 troops into battle. Perhaps the state's biggest role during the Civil War was the manufacturing of much needed rifles, ammunition, and uniforms, which inevitably signaled Connecticut's emergence as a manufacturing giant.

The state continued to donate its manufacturing resources to the war efforts of both World Wars, and the state prospered by supplying munitions, weapons and other supplies. Manufacturing began to decline during the 1970's as the growth of the financial, real estate, insurance, and service industries took root. Wealth was limited to the suburbs however, while central cities such as Bridgeport have failed to the point of bankruptcy. The 1990's saw the development of Native American casinos, which have since supplanted defence industries as the state's main economic engine.

## Important Genealogical Dates in Connecticut History

**1633** – Dutch fort and trading post founded at site of present-day Hartford

**1634** – First English settlers from Massachusetts arrive and form settlements at Windsor, Hartford, and Wethersfield

**1637** – towns separate from Massachusetts and form the Connecticut Colony

**1646** – New London founded

**1662** – Receives charter as royal corporate colony

**1665** – New Haven unites with Connecticut Colony

**1740** – majority of the state organized into towns

**1777** – British forces raid Danbury

**1788** – Statehood

**1818** – State Constitution written

**1838** – New Hartford railroad completed

## Famous Battles Fought in Connecticut

Several battles between the Revolutionary forces and the British took place in Connecticut. Additionally there are many accounts of the battles fought during the **Pequot War**. These battle accounts can be very effective in uncovering the military records of your ancestor. They can tell you what regiments fought in which battles, and often include the names and ranks of many officers and enlisted men. Following are some of the most famous battles fought in Connecticut and links to useful information about them.

**Pequot War**:http://pequotwar.org/

Important Revolutionary War Battles fought in Connecticut were:

**Battle of Ridgefield**, 1777:
http://www.ridgefieldct.org/content/42/249/1077.aspx

**Battle of Norwalk**, 1779:
http://celebratethepastinc.com/Patriot_Days.html

**Battle of New Haven**, 1779;
http://www.richmangalleries.com/Revolutionary%20War/battle%20of%20new%20haven.htm

**Battle of Groton Heights**, 1781:
http://www.battleofgrotonheights.com/

**Common Connecticut Genealogical Issues and Resources to Overcome Them**

**Boundary Changes**: Boundary changes are a common obstacle when researching Connecticut ancestors. You could be searching for an ancestor's record in one county when in fact it is stored in a different one due to historical county boundary changes. The **Atlas of Historical County Boundaries** can help you to overcome that problem. It provides a chronological listing of every boundary change that has occurred in the history of Connecticut.

**Atlas of Historical County Boundaries**: http://publications.newberry.org/ahcbp/documents/CT_Consolidated _Chronology.htm#Consolidated_Chronology

**Name Changes**: Surname changes, variations, and misspellings can complicate genealogical research. It is important to check all spelling variations. Soundex, a program that indexes names by sound, is a useful first step, but you can't rely on it completely as some name variations result in different Soundex codes. The surnames could be different, but the first name may be different too. You can also find records filed under initials, middle names, and nicknames as well, so you will need to **get creative with surname variations** and spellings in order to cover all the possibilities. For help with surname variations read our instructional article on **How to Use Soundex**.

**get creative with surname variations**: http://obituarieshelp.org/blog/?p=634

**How to Use Soundex**: http://obituarieshelp.org/blog/?p=505

## Connecticut Genealogical Organizations and Archives

Genealogical resources include not only records, but the organizations that house them, or can direct you to them. These institutions include: *Archives, Libraries, Genealogical Societies, Family History Centers, Universities, Churches, and Museums.*

Following are links to their websites, their physical addresses, and a summary of the records you can find there.

Archives

**Department of Public Health State Vital Records Office** – Birth records 1897-present, Death Records: 1897 – present, Death Indexes: 1949 – present, Marriage Records: 1897 – present Marriage Indexes: 1959 – present

CT Department of Public Health
Vital Records Office
410 Capitol Ave. MS#11VRS
Hartford, CT 06134-0308
Tel: (860) 509-7700
Fax: (860) 509-7964

**Department of Public Health State Vital Records Office**:
http://www.ct.gov/dph/cwp/view.asp?a=3132&q=388130&dphNav=
|46940|

**Connecticut State Library (holds the State Archives)** - pre-1897 vital records, census reports, maps, historical newspapers, Civil War records, Revolutionary War records, probate records

231 Capitol Avenue
Hartford, CT 06106
Tel: 860-757-6500

**Connecticut State Library**:
http://www.ctstatelibrary.org/topics/history-genealogy

**University of Connecticut University Libraries** – Colonial Connecticut Records, 1636-1776

University of Connecticut Libraries
369 Fairfield Way
Storrs, CT 06269
Tel:860 486-2518

**University of Connecticut University Libraries**:
http://www.colonialct.uconn.edu/

## Connecticut Genealogical and Historical Societies

Genealogical and historical societies have access to extensive catalogues of genealogical data. They are also able to offer expert guidance for genealogical researchers. Many members are professional genealogists who are most willing to share their expertise in finding ancestors.

**Connecticut Historical Society** – passenger and immigration lists, military lists, census reports, manuscripts, vital records extracts, periodicals

One Elizabeth Street
Hartford, CT 06105
Tel: (860) 236-5621

**Connecticut Historical Society**: http://www.chs.org/familyhistory

**Connecticut Society of Genealogists, Inc** – wide variety of genealogical resources
175 Maple Street
East Hartford, CT 06118-2634
or
PO Box 435
Glastonbury, CT 06033-0435

**Connecticut Society of Genealogists, Inc**: http://www.csginc.org/

**Danbury Museum and Historical Society**-Historical newspapers, city directories, family surname files, early records including vital statistics, land and census information, cemetery transcriptions and military history

43 Main Street
Danbury, CT 06810
(203) 743-5200

**Danbury Museum and Historical Society**: http://www.danburyhistorical.org/

**Amity and Woodbridge Historical Society**
Thomas Darling House
1907 Litchfield Turnpike
Woodbridge, CT 06525
Tel: (203) 387-2823

**Amity and Woodbridge Historical Society**:
http://www.woodbridgehistory.org/

**Killingly Historical and Genealogical Society, Inc.**
196 Main Street
PO Box 6000
Danielson, CT 06239
(860) 779-7250

**Killingly Historical and Genealogical Society, Inc.**:
http://www.killinglyhistory.org/

**Polish Genealogical Society of Connecticut and the Northeast** –
cemetery records, immigration records, surnames indexes, church
directories, gazetteers, marriage records

8 Lyle Road
New Britain, CT 06053-2104
Tel: 860-229-8873
Email: pgsctne@yahoo.com

**Polish Genealogical Society of Connecticut and the Northeast**:
http://www.pgsctne.org/

**Jewish Genealogical Society of Connecticut** – surnames lists,
cemeteries lists, histories, passenger lists, passenger arrivals

134 Newfield St.
Middletown, CT 06457
Email: info@jgsct-jewish-genealogy.org

**Jewish Genealogical Society of Connecticut**: http://www.jgsct-
jewish-genealogy.org/

Connecticut Family History Centers

The Family History Centers run by the LDS Church offer free access to billions of genealogical records for free to the general public. They also provide classes on genealogy and one-on-one assistance to inexperienced family historians. Here you will find a **Complete Listing of Connecticut Family History Centers**.

**Complete Listing of Connecticut Family History Centers**:
https://familysearch.org/locations/centerlocator

**Additional Connecticut Genealogical Resources**

Connecticut Mailing Lists

Mailing lists are internet based facilities that use email to distribute a single message to all who subscribe to it. When information on a particular surname, new records, or any other important genealogy information related to the mailing list topic becomes available, the subscribers are alerted to it. Joining a mailing list is an excellent way to stay up to date on Connecticut genealogy research topics. Rootsweb have an extensive listing of **Connecticut Mailing Lists** on a variety of topics.

**Connecticut Mailing Lists**:
http://lists.rootsweb.ancestry.com/index/usa/CT/misc.html

Connecticut Message Boards

A message board is another internet based facility where people can post questions about a specific genealogy topic and have it answered by other genealogists. If you have questions about a surname, record type, or research topic, you can post your question and other researchers and genealogists will help you with the answer. Be sure to check back regularly, as the answers are not emailed to you. The Connecticut message boards at **Rootsweb** are completely free to use.

**Rootsweb**:
http://boards.rootsweb.com/localities.northam.usa.states/mb.ashx

Connecticut Newspapers and Periodicals

Many genealogy periodicals and historical newspapers contain reprinted copies of family genealogies, transcripts of family Bible records, information about local records and archives, census indexes, church records, queries, land records, obituaries, court records, cemetery records, and wills. The following sites have historical Connecticut newspapers and periodicals that you can search online or on-site.

**Connecticut State Library** - 100,000 pages
of newspapers published in Connecticut between 1836 and 1922, Hartford Courant 1764-1922

**Connecticut State Library**:
http://www.ctstatelibrary.org/topics/history-genealogy

**Danbury Museum and Historical Society-** historical newspapers from around the state.

**Danbury Museum and Historical Society:** http://www.danburyhistorical.org/

**Silas Bronson Library** – Connecticut and New England Genealogy and historical periodicals

267 Grand Street
Waterbury, CT 06702
Tel: 203-574-8226
Email: sbl-refdesk@waterburyct.org

**Silas Bronson Library**:
http://www.bronsonlibrary.org/filestorage/1521/1547/periodicals.pdf

**NewspaperArchive.com** – largest online database of historical newspapers in the world.

**NewspaperArchive.com**: http://newspaperarchive.com/

## Historical Connecticut Maps and Gazetteers

Maps are an integral part of genealogical research. They help us to locate landmarks, towns, cities, parishes, states, provinces, waterways and roads and streets. They also help us to determine when and where boundary changes might have taken place, and give us a visualization of the area we're researching in. For locating place names, a gazetteer is the best possible resource for any genealogist. Gazetteers are also sometimes called "place name dictionaries", and can help you to locate the area in which you need to conduct research. Below are links to the maps and gazetteers for research in Connecticut.

**Peabody GNIS Service – Connecticut**:
http://peabody.research.yale.edu/cgi-bin/Query.GNIS?ST=Connecticut&SU=1

**Color Landform Atlas – Connecticut**:
http://fermi.jhuapl.edu/states/ct_0.html

**1985 U.S. Atlas**: http://www.livgenmi.com/1895/CT/

**Connecticut Hometown Locator**:
http://connecticut.hometownlocator.com/

Connecticut City Directories

City directories are similar to telephone directories in that they list the residents of a particular area. The difference though is what is important to genealogists, and that is they pre-date telephone directories. You can find an ancestor's information such as their street address, place of employment, occupation, or the name of their spouse. A one-stop-shop for finding city directories in Connecticut is the **Connecticut Online Historical Directories** which contains a listing of every available city and historical directory related to Connecticut.

**Connecticut Online Historical Directories**:
https://sites.google.com/site/onlinedirectorysite/Home/usa/ct

**Danbury Museum and Historical Society**-Historical newspapers, city directories, family surname files, early records including vital statistics, land and census information, cemetery transcriptions and military history

43 Main Street
Danbury, CT 06810
(203) 743-5200

**Danbury Museum and Historical Society:** http://www.danburyhistorical.org/

# Connecticut Genealogical Records

Birth, Death, Marriage and Divorce Records – Birth, death, and marriage records are the most basic, yet most important records attached to your ancestor. They are generally referred to as vital records as they record vital life events. The reason for their importance is that they not only place your ancestor in a specific place at a definite time, but potentially connect the individual to other relatives. Below is a list of repositories and websites where you can find Connecticut vital records

**Department of Public Health State Vital Records Office** – Birth records 1897-present, Marriage Records: 1897 – present, Marriage Indexes: 1959 – present

Mailing Address:
CT Department of Public Health
State Office of Vital Records
410 Capitol Ave.  MS#11VRS
P.O. Box 340308
Hartford, CT  06134-0308

**Department of Public Health State Vital Records Office**:
http://www.ct.gov/dph/cwp/view.asp?a=3132&q=388132

**Connecticut State Library** - pre-1897 vital records

231 Capitol Avenue
Hartford, CT 06106
Tel: 860-757-6500

**Connecticut State Library**:
http://www.ctstatelibrary.org/topics/history-genealogy

**Danbury Museum and Historical Society**-early records including vital statistics

43 Main Street
Danbury, CT 06810
(203) 743-5200

**Danbury Museum and Historical Society**: http://www.danburyhistorical.org/

**Family Search** - Connecticut, Births and Christenings, 1649-1906, Connecticut, Death Index, 1949-2001, Connecticut Deaths and Burials, 1772-1934,Connecticut Divorce Index, 1968-1997, Connecticut Marriage Index, 1959-2001,Connecticut Marriages, 1729-1867

**Family Search**:
https://familysearch.org/search/collection/list#uri=http://www.family search.org/searchapi/search/collection/1674736

## Census Reports

Census records are among the most important genealogical documents for placing your ancestor in a particular place at a specific time. Like BDM records, they can also lead you to other ancestors, particularly those who were living under the authority of the head of household.

Connecticut census records exist from 1670 and many images and indexes can be viewed online. Following are the best places to find Connecticut census records.

**New Horizons Genealogy** - a transcribed listing of 1544 heads of household and 824 freemen from information found in household, landowner, church, estate, tax, and freeman lists between the years 1660 and 1673.

**New Horizons Genealogy**:
http://www.newhorizonsgenealogicalservices.com/1670-ct-state.htm

**Yale University Library** - A Return of the number of inhabitants in the state of Connecticut, February 1, 1782, includes Native Americans and Negroes

**Yale University Library**:
http://orbis.library.yale.edu/vwebv/holdingsInfo?searchId=622&rec Count=50&recPointer=0&bibId=7393157

**Archive.org** - census of Newington, Connecticut, 1909 available to read online or by download

**Archive.org**: http://archive.org/details/censusofnewingto00will

**Connecticut State Library** - Census of New London County 1790

**Connecticut State Library**:
http://www.consuls.org/record=b2419621~S1

**Family Link** – census of 1790-1949

**Family Link**: http://www.familylink.com/contentview.aspx?p=ct

**US Census Bureau** – heads of household listing for 1790 Connecticut

**US Census Bureau**:
http://www.census.gov/prod/www/abs/decennial/1790.htm

**U.S National Archives** – Federal census records on microfilm available from 1790 to 1940.

**U.S National Archives**: http://www.archives.gov/research/census/

Connecticut Church Records

Church and synagogue records are a valuable resource, especially for baptisms, marriages, and burials that took place before 1900. You will need to at least have an idea of your ancestor's religious denomination, and in most cases you will have to visit a brick and mortar establishment to view them.

Most church records are kept by the individual church, although in some denominations, records are placed in a regional archive or maintained at the diocesan level. Local Historical Societies are sometimes the repository for the state's older church records. Below are links archives that maintain church records, as well as a few databases that can be viewed online.

The **Family History Library** contains many church records from a variety of denominations on microfilm.

**Family History Library**:
http://familysearch.org/learn/wiki/en/Family_History_Library

The **Connecticut State Library** holds the records of more than 600 Connecticut churches

**Connecticut State Library**: http://www.ctstatelibrary.org/church

**Central Repositories for Denominational Records**

Baptist

**American Baptist Historical Society**
American Baptist Historical Society
3001 Mercer University Drive
Atlanta, GA 30341
Tel: 678-547-6680

**American Baptist Historical Society**:
http://abhsarchives.org/about/

Congregational

**Connecticut Historical Society**
1 Elizabeth Street
Hartford, CT 06105
Tel: (860) 236-5621
Fax: (860) 236-2664

**Connecticut Historical Society**: http://www.chs.org/

**The Congregational Library**
14 Beacon Street
Boston, MA 02108-3704
Tel: (617) 523-0470
Fax: (617) 523-0491

**The Congregational Library**:
http://www.congregationallibrary.org/

Episcopal

**Episcopal Diocese of Connecticut**
135 Asylum Avenue
Hartford, CT 06105-2295
Tel: (860) 233-4481
Fax: (860) 523-1410

**Episcopal Diocese of Connecticut**:
https://www.ctepiscopal.org/default.asp

Methodist

**United Methodist Archives Center**
Drew University Library
P.O. Box 127
Madison, NJ 07940
Tel: (201) 408-3189

**United Methodist Archives Center**:
http://www.gcah.org/site/pp.aspx?c=ghKJI0PHIoE&b=3590193

Moravian

**The Moravian Archives**
41 West Locust Street
Bethlehem, Pennsylvania 18018
United States of America
Tel: (610) 866-3255
Fax: (610) 866-9210

**The Moravian Archives**: http://www.moravianchurcharchives.org/

Roman Catholic

**Diocese of Bridgeport**
238 Jewett Avenue
Bridgeport, CT 06606
Tel: (203) 416-1354

**Diocese of Bridgeport**:
http://www.bridgeportdiocese.com/welcome.shtml

**Diocese of Norwich**
201 Broadway P.O. Box 587
Norwich, CT 06360
Tel: (860) 887-9294
Fax: (860) 886-1670

**Diocese of Norwich**: http://www.norwichdiocese.org/

**Diocese of Hartford**
134 Farmington Avenue
Hartford, CT 06103
Tel: (860) 541-6491
Fax: (860) 541-6309

**Diocese of Hartford**: http://www.archdioceseofhartford.org/

## Connecticut Military Records

More than 40 million Americans have participated in some time of war service since America was colonized. The chance of finding your ancestor amongst those records is exceptionally high. Military records can even reveal individuals who never actually served, such as those who registered for the two World Wars but were never called to duty.

Below are a number of links to websites and archives that contain Connecticut military records.

**New Horizons Genealogy** – 1813 Pension List, Connecticut Pensioners Of The United States, 1818, 1832 Military Pensions List – searchable by county and including names of officers and enlisted men who had served for two years

**New Horizons Genealogy**:
http://www.newhorizonsgenealogicalservices.com/1832-pension-list-ct.htm

**Connecticut State Library** – Colonial War records, 1675-1774, Revolutionary War records, Civil War records

**Connecticut State Library**:
http://www.ctstatelibrary.org/search/node/military%20records

**U.S. National Archives** – WWI Draft registration cards, casualties lists, WWI and WWII service records, Korean War records, Vietnam War records, Civil War and Spanish-American War records, and casualties lists.

**U.S. National Archives**:
http://www.archives.gov/research/military/veterans/online.html

**US Department of Veterans Affairs Nationwide Gravesite Locator** – includes information on veterans and their family members buried in veterans and military cemeteries having a government grave marker.

**US Department of Veterans Affairs Nationwide Gravesite Locator**: http://gravelocator.cem.va.gov/

**United States Index to Indian Wars Pension Files, 1892-1926** – military pension records of soldiers who fought in the Indian Wars between 1817 and 1898

**United States Index to Indian Wars Pension Files, 1892-1926**: https://familysearch.org/search/collection/1979427

**United States Mexican War Pension Index, 1887-1926** - index to Mexican War pension files for service between 1846 and 1848

**United States Mexican War Pension Index, 1887-1926**: https://familysearch.org/search/collection/1979390

**Civil War Soldiers Service Records** - Service records for both Union and Confederate soldiers indexed by soldier's name, rank, and unit.

**Civil War Soldier Service Records**: http://go.fold3.com/civilwar_records/

## Connecticut Cemetery Records

As convenient as it is to search cemetery records online, keep in mind that there are a few disadvantages over visiting a cemetery in person. They are:

- Tombstone information is not always accurately transcribed
- The arrangement of the graves in a cemetery can be crucial as family members are often buried next to each other or in the same grave. This arrangement is not always preserved in the alphabetical indexes that are found online.

With that information in mind, the following websites have databases that can be searched online for Connecticut Cemetery records.

**Connecticut Tombstone Transcription Project** - death and burial records

**Connecticut Tombstone Transcription Project**: http://www.usgwtombstones.org/connecticut/connecti.html

**Danbury Museum and Historical Society-**Cemetery transcriptions

43 Main Street
Danbury, CT 06810
(203) 743-5200

**Danbury Museum and Historical Society:** http://www.danburyhistorical.org/

**The Hale Collection** - cemetery inscriptions (1640s-1930s)

**The Hale Collection**: http://www.ctstatelibrary.org/subjectguides/hale-collection-cemetery-inscriptions

**African American Cemeteries Online** – African American, slave, and Native American cemetery records

**African American Cemeteries Online**: http://africanamericancemeteries.com/

**Access Genealogy** – huge database of Connecticut cemetery record transcriptions

**Access Genealogy**: http://www.accessgenealogy.com/cemetery/connecticut.htm

**Find a Grave** – over 100 million grave records can be searched on this site. Search can be conducted by name, location, or cemetery name.

**Find a Grave**: http://www.findagrave.com/

**Interment.net** - A free online database containing approximately 4 million cemetery records from around the world.

**Interment.net**: http://www.interment.net/

**Billion Graves** – as the name implies, you can search a billion records including headstone photos, transcriptions, cemetery records, and grave locations.

**Billion Graves**: http://billiongraves.com/pages/search/index.php#cemetery

Connecticut Obituaries

Obituaries can reveal a wealth about our ancestor and other relatives. You can search our **Connecticut Newspaper Obituaries Listings** from hundreds of Connecticut newspapers online for free.

**Connecticut Newspaper Obituaries Listings**: http://obituarieshelp.org/connecticut_newspaper_obituaries.html

## Connecticut Wills and Probate Records

The documents found in a probate packet may include a complete inventory of a person's estate, newspaper entries, witness testimony, a copy of a will, list of debtors and creditors, names of executors or trustees, names of heirs. They can not only tell you about the ancestor you're currently researching, but lead to other ancestors. Most of these records must be accessed at a county court or clerk's office, but some can be found online as well. You can obtain copies of the original probate records by writing to the county clerk.

**Connecticut State Library** – early Colonial probate records dating from 1635 to early 20th century.

**Connecticut State Library**: http://www.cslib.org/probintr.htm

**Connecticut Archives** – estates of deceased persons, 1649-1820

**Connecticut Archives**:
http://cslib.contentdm.oclc.org/cdm/ref/collection/p128501coll3/id/11233

**Connecticut Probate Courts** – directory of county probate courts to which you can write for records

**Connecticut Probate Courts**:
http://www.ctprobate.gov/Pages/Welcome.aspx

## Connecticut Immigration and Naturalization Records

The naturalization process generated many types of records, including petitions, declarations of intention, and oaths of allegiance. These records can provide family historians with information such as a person's birth date and place of birth, immigration year, marital status, spouse information, occupation, witnesses' names and addresses, and more.

**National Archives New England Region (Boston)** – naturalization and immigration records for Connecticut from 1842-1973

The National Archives at Boston
380 Trapelo Road
Waltham, Massachusetts
02452-6399

Toll Free Telephone: (866) 406-2379
Telephone: (781) 663-0144
Fax: (781) 663-0154
E-mail: boston.archives@nara.gov

**National Archives New England Region (Boston)**:
http://www.archives.gov/boston/public/genealogy.html

**Connecticut State Library** – Naturalization records from 1791-1906

**Connecticut State Library**: http://www.cslib.org/natural.htm#2

Connecticut Native American Records

**Access Genealogy** – Native American census records, tribal histories, and much more

**Access Genealogy**: http://www.accessgenealogy.com/native/

**Midwest Genealogy Center** – a wide variety of records from the vast majority of Native American tribes in the United States on microfilm

Midwest Genealogy Center
3440 S. Lee's Summit Road
Independence, Missouri

**Midwest Genealogy Center**:
http://www.mymcpl.org/_uploaded_resources/MGC-micronatamer.pdf

The **National Archives** - information about American Indians who maintained their ties to Federally-recognized Tribes (1830-1970):
http://www.archives.gov/research/native-americans/

**Bureau of Indian Affairs**

**Bureau of Indian Affairs**: http://www.bia.gov/

**American Indians Records Repository** - records dating from the 1700s including trust, education and other historic Indian Affairs records

American Indian Records Repository
Meritex Enterprises
17501 West 98th Street
Lenexa, KS 66219
Phone: 913-888-0601

**American Indians Records Repository:**
http://www.doi.gov/ost/records_mgmt/american-indian-records-repository.cfm

# Missing Matriarchs – Resources for Researching Female Connecticut Ancestors

Looking for female ancestors requires an adjustment of how we view traditional records sources. A woman's identity was often under that of her husband, and often individual records for them can be difficult to locate. The following resources are effective in locating female ancestors in Connecticut where traditional records may not reveal them.

Marriage and Divorce Records

The earliest marriage records were recorded by the towns and often mixed with land records. It wasn't until 1849 that town and probate clerks were ordered to record marriages. In addition to original town records, the following indexes can be found at the Connecticut State Library:

1. Barbour Index to Vital records, (film 0002887 ff.)
2. Hale Collection of Vital records (film 0003076 ff.)

Divorces were first recorded in the General Court of Connecticut Colony, and in the Court of Magistrates in New Haven Colony. The Superior Court was given jurisdiction in 1711, and later records are held by the Clerk of the Superior Court in the county where the divorce was granted. Many records of divorce have been filmed at the Connecticut State Library and are as follows:

- Fairfield County, 1720-1799 (film 1673219 ff.)
- Hartford County, 1725-1849 (film 1637917 ff.)
- Litchfield County, 1752-1922 (film 1664674 ff.)
- Middlesex County, 1786-1797 (film 1639454 ff.)
- New Haven County, 1712-1899 (film 1672069 ff.)
- New London County, 1719-1875 (film 1638067 ff.)
- Tolland County, 1787-1910 (film 1637443 ff.)
- Windham County, 1726-1907 (film 1638582 ff.)

Bibliographies

- *A Sampler of Lifestyles: Womanhood and Youth in Colonial Lyme*, Mary Sterling Bakke (Advocate Press, 1976)
- *Property and Kinship: Inheritance in Early Connecticut, 1750-1820,* Toby L. Ditz (Princeton University Press, 1986)
- *Connecticut Women in the Revolutionary Era,* Catherine Fennelly (American Revolution Bicentennial Commission for Connecticut, 1975)
- *Connecticut's Divorce Mechanism, 1639-1969,* Henry S. Cohn (American Journal of Legal History 14 (1970) pgs 25-54)
- *Connecticut Sources for Family Historians and Genealogists,* Kip Sperry (Everton Publishers, 1980)

## Selected Resources for Connecticut Women's History

Institute for Study of Women and Gender
University of Connecticut
U Box 181
417 Whitney Rd
Storrs, CT 06269-1181

Litchfield Historical Society
South and East Streets
PO Box 385
Litchfield, CT 06759-0385

Prudence Crandall Museum
PO Box 47
Canterbury, CT 06331

## Common Connecticut Surnames

The following surnames are among the most common in Connecticut. The list is by no means exhaustive. If your surname doesn't appear in the list it doesn't mean that you have no Connecticut connections, only that your surname may be less common.

Abel, Ackart, Adams, Alford, Allen, Alling, Allyn, Alvord, Bancroft, Barber, Barker, Barnard, Barnes, Bartlet, Bartlett, Baysey, Beach, Beckwith, Beers, Bemis, Bennett, Benton, Bird, Bishop, Bissell, Brown, Buell, Burr, Carter, Case, Chapman, Clark, Coe, Cornish, Cornwel, Crow, Curtis, Dibble, Dickerman, Dickinson, Dill, Drake, Eggleston, Ellsworth, Eno, Foote, Frisbie, Gaylord, Gilbert, Gillette, Goodwin, Grant, Gray, Griffin, Griswold, Hall, Harris, Harrison, Hayes, Holcombe, Hoskins, Hubbard, Hubbell, Hull, Humphrey, Judd, Judson, Keeler, Linsley, Loomis, Lord, Marshfield, Merrell, Mills, Moore, Morris, Northrop, Northrup, Olmstead, Osborn, Peck, Pettibone, Phelps, Pinney, Prudden, Ranney, Reed, Rogers, Rose, Sanford, Scott, Seeley, Shepard, Smith, Spencer, Starr, Stebbins, Stilson, Thompson, Thrall, Wilcox, Williams, Winston, Winton, Woodford, Wright

About the Author

Gary L. Morris worked from 2009 to 2014 as a professional researcher for a major player in the genealogy field. After tracing his family lineage back to 1683, he found that genealogy could be an expensive undertaking. As such, has decided to publish these helpful guides to share the valuable free information he has discovered during his career to help others trace their family lineages as inexpensively as possible. An avid genealogist himself, he hopes you will find this guide factual, thorough, helpful, and most of all, effective in helping you to find your family members.

# Notes

# Notes

www.ingramcontent.com/pod-product-compliance
Lightning Source LLC
Chambersburg PA
CBHW061930280526
45787CB00004B/1553